Flour, Water, and Everything Else

How to bake like you know what you're doing

Zachary Ahlers © 2019

My sincerest thanks to those who have enjoyed my baking,
And my sincerest apologies to those who have not.

The whole point

I hate cookbooks. They give you a list of ingredients you'll probably need to buy solely for this purpose, a set of precise steps using unexplained jargon, and no real way to know whether or not it turned out "correctly". Then, if it doesn't turn out like you think it should, they give you a giant middle finger full of thinly veiled conceit as they "encourage" you to try again. And even if you've done everything correctly, you still end up with something the author enjoys but you might hate with no way to modify the final product.

This is not a cookbook. I won't include a single recipe. Instead, my goal is to give you an idea of what baking is, what the ingredients contribute to the final product, and what changes you can make to get the result you want. I'm not going to lie to you, baking is a stupidly precise process. Changing one ingredient or step by 10% can either do absolutely nothing, change the texture drastically, make it taste inedible, or explode over the baking dish and coat your oven with what you had once hoped would be a delicious birthday carrot cake. Centuries have gone into figuring out what works, and most recipes (especially from name-brand chefs or companies) follow those traditions closely, but that shouldn't prevent you from adjusting them to your tastes or needs. Why did the recipe call for 3 whole eggs *and* an extra egg yolk? What if I'm allergic to eggs? Do I really have to wait two hours for the dough to rise, only to punch it down again? Why do I have to add a quarter of a teaspoon of salt into this giant bowl of flour? Can I cook my cake at a higher temperature to get it done faster? Why do I keep asking rhetorical questions when I assume that this book will answer some most of them?

This book is a collection of the things that I think you should know to help you bake. I don't want to fill it with complicated exposition and chemistry, but when I feel it's necessary I'll include an endnote with some additional information on the topic at hand. If your quest is to bake a perfect loaf of bread, drop this book and become a baker. Enroll in culinary school. If your goal is to bake *better* than what can be done by following a recipe, maybe these tools will help you too.

"Baking is wonderful!
It's like science for hungry people!"
-Hannelore Ellicott-Chatham

An Understanding of Dough

To start making a dough all you need are flour and water. That's it. Everything else is a modifier. If your recipe doesn't call for flour or water, then why are you even reading this book? There are only a few topics that are truly important to making dough, specifically gluten formation (chewiness), leavening (air pockets), and modifying ingredients (like sugar, eggs, and salt).

What the hell is gluten?

Gluten, what some consider to be Satan incarnate, is simpler than people make it out to be. Flour[1] contains proteins that like to stick together. When they bond and form long chains and networks, we call those networks **gluten**. Think of it like a tangle of ultra-thin elastic bands running throughout the dough, giving structure to what would otherwise be a thick starch paste. It can cause problems in people with celiac disease or gluten sensitivity (which some

---

[1] This book only covers wheat flour, other flours generate differing levels of gluten and some (like exotic rice, almond, or coconut flours) form none at all.

assholes think is a made-up disease that people use for attention), but otherwise is harmless and an important substance to understand when baking.

Gluten makes things chewy and springy, so it's important to know when you want a lot and when you only want a little. French bread? Lots of gluten. Pie crust? Flaky products should be lower in gluten. Croissants? Better believe there's a whole lotta gluten in there. Brownies? Who the fuck wants a tough chewy brownie?

There are 4 things[2] that influence the amount of gluten in your dough: kneading time, and the protein, water, and fat contents.

Kneading

In order for proteins to form into gluten, they first need to actually come into contact with each other. This is what kneading does, it gives the proteins a chance to mingle before hooking up, like a baking chemistry version of Tinder. When a recipe tells you to mix ingredients "until incorporated", what they're saying is that they don't want an excessive amount of gluten forming from overmixing. On the other hand, for a chewy and hearty hearth bread, you'll want to knead the hell out of it to bulk up the gluten. If your recipe calls for it, DON'T SKIP THE KNEADING STEP. Take a breath, stretch out your wrists, take a

---

[2] As with so many things in this book, there are far more than just 4 contributors to gluten formation (including variety of wheat, water hardness, pH, and presence of gluten-busting enzymes), but if I covered all of them I would end up writing a textbook.

fortifying sip of your favorite wine, and dive into the dough.

When your dough is thin or watery it's easy enough to mix with a spatula, whisk, or whatever you have on hand, but when your dough is thick enough to hold its own shape and can be picked up as a single piece, then it can be kneaded. Flatten the dough a bit, then fold it onto itself. Press it back into another flatish shape and fold again, in a different direction from the first time. That's all kneading is, repeated flattening, folding, and pressing. Start by checking to see if the dough sticks to whatever it touches. If it does, congrats on your first dough-countertop hybrid. You might need to let the dough sit or chill in the fridge for a little bit to make it less sticky. You can also coat your hands and the kneading surface in a little flour to keep it from sticking, but too much and you'll dry out your dough. Make sure to flip the dough every now and again so that one section of the dough doesn't fuse to your work surface. If the dough starts to tear, channel your inner Bob Ross and try to knead less aggressively, and if the dough becomes tough to work, you can surf Facebook for a few minutes while the gluten relaxes before trying again.

If everything goes wrong, e.g. it sticks like hell, tears apart, or starts spouting profanities in a foreign language (especially German), feel free to scrape it up into a mixing bowl, punch it back into a single piece, and throw it into the fridge for an hour while you calm down with your consumable of choice. This will give the dough time to think about what it's done, and it will still be there when you're ready to try again. Time heals all things, unless you're trying to minimize the gluten in your dough, in which case time is your bitter enemy that will stop at nothing to destroy you. The longer the dough is allowed to set (especially if it is occasionally kneaded/mixed) the more gluten will form.

Flour Type

Ever wonder what the difference is between all the flours on the shelf in the baking aisle? I'm not talking about brands, I mean shit like "All-purpose" flour, "pastry" flour, or "bread" flour. Short answer: they have different protein content. For the long answer, re-read the last sentence slower. The more protein in the flour, the more gluten that can form. Bread flour has as many gluten forming proteins as you can get,[3] while pastry/cake flour has about half as much. All-Purpose flour, as its name would imply, falls in the middle and will usually serve well enough for whatever you're making. Using the right type of flour isn't always vital, but is probably the simplest step to starting your dough off on the right foot.

Another note for the health-nuts out there: Whole wheat flour *sucks* at forming gluten. Regular flour is made from only a portion of the wheat kernel, the portion highest in starch and low in fiber. Whole wheat flour uses, you guessed it, the whole kernel of

---

[3] At least, as much protein as you can get with the standard milling techniques in use today. You can also get "vital gluten flour", which is specifically made to have a stupidly high gluten content, using more complex techniques. If your recipe calls for this, there is nothing else that can give you more gluten.

wheat. This introduces tiny shards of the hard shell that slice and dice the gluten as it tries to form. Using a little is fine, but a large amount will seriously screw up your dish if you don't account for it.

Water Content

If you don't think that water is necessary for the formation of gluten, try this little experiment. Pour some flour in a bowl. Notice, it crumbles and falls apart when you touch it. Bet you feel silly now, huh?

In order for gluten to form, it must be suspended in water. Water is the Goldilocks of gluten formation: too little and you have a dry mess that crumbles if you look at it sternly, too much and you have a liquid dough that can only form gluten after an absurd amount of mixing. But a moderate amount of water (50-80% as much water as flour, by weight) will allow the dough to form into a solid ball, for large amounts gluten to form, and to produce enough deliciously chewy bread to satisfy three hungry bears.

Fat Content

A lot of recipes call for "shortening" to be used. The question I had for most of my life was: What is shortening, and why does it have such a stupid name? Well fear not, because after tireless research (5 minutes on Wikipedia) I now know the answer, and I'm willing to share it with you: Shortening is solid fat. That's it. Butter, margarine, lard, and beef tallow are all types of shortening (though Butter and Margarine also contain water). Why is fat important in baking? Because fat *inhibits* the formation of gluten. In more scientific terms, while water allows for chains of gluten throughout the dough to get longer, fat *shortens* them. And thus, "shortening" was what was used to keep the dough from getting too chewy and stretchy, giving us the texture we want in tender cookies, flaky pie crusts, or crumbly brownies. This shortening effect is especially effective if the fat is mixed into the flour before water is added, as the thin layer of fat on each particle of flour acts like a tiny shell that minimizes contact with other flour particles.

It's worth noting that any fat (not just solid fat) has the same effect on gluten, so olive oil will do the same thing as lard. However, adding a solid shortening will help the dough keep its shape if you need to mold the dough into something, while liquid fats will do the opposite.

Inflating your dough

Unless you want your pastries to have the final density of fudge, you'll want to have air in them. We do this by **leavening** our dough, which adds air to the final product through chemical, mechanical, or biological means. The primary ways of leavening are: yeast, chemical leavening, air, and uneven steam production.

Chemical Leavening

In my experience, chemical leavening is the simplest, though it is limited in where it can be applied. Ever hear of baking soda[4]? That's a chemical leavener. When mixed with a weak acid and heated, it produces bubbles of gas that fill the dough as it bakes. It's commonly mixed with a solid long-lasting acid (typically cream of tartar) and sold as **baking powder**, which can be mixed directly into the dough. So if chemical leavening is so easy, why do we use other methods? I'm glad you asked, inquisitive hypothetical! Two reasons: First, baking soda is great at making tons of tiny bubbles, but not so great at making the huge bubbles we get in artisan bread. Second, it has a distinct acidic taste to it that would be out of place in a lot of pastries.

Yeast

Yeast is a living organism that we willingly introduce into our food. It's been used for hundreds of years to make bread, and has such a distinctive taste that if you said that something tasted "bready", anyone listening would understand. Yeast has the sole desire to consume sugar and to excrete alcohol and carbon dioxide gas. This makes it useful in the brewing industry (for the alcohol), but also in baking (for the carbon dioxide). Unlike chemical leavening, yeast will produce gas at room temperature, which has the delightful side effect of letting us wait until the dough is as fluffy and big as we want it before we throw it in the oven. On the other hand, yeast has a downside: it's alive, and surprisingly easy to kill. There are only a few things to pay attention to for yeast to be a good leavener:

---

[4] Also called Sodium Bicarbonate, or bicarbonate of soda.

- Yeast requires water to live comfortably. You can't drown yeast, but if the dough is too dry it will struggle.
- Yeast requires sugar to eat, but too much will hurt it. There is a little sugar already present in flour, but you can add a dash more to give it a boost. Once you get into the dessert category with a lot of sugar, the yeast will have a difficult time and it may be better to consider a different leavener.
- Salt will kill yeast if you add too much.
- Yeast can die of old age. If the yeast in your cabinet is old, it may already be dead[5].
- Yeast thrives at room temperature or slightly warmer. Too hot or too cold both cause problems[6].

Like any organism, yeast requires patience to work well. If you're scrambling to bake something for a potluck in an hour, don't make anything with yeast in it or it'll rise slowly out of pure spite. Most recipes with yeast call for a **proofing** step, which means that you wait until the dough has doubled in volume

---

[5] You can test your yeast by adding 1 tsp of sugar and a quarter cup of warm (~100 degrees Fahrenheit) water to half a tablespoon of yeast. If the surface gets foamy after 10 minutes the yeast is alive and well, the longer you have to wait for bubbles the less active the yeast is.

[6] Cold dough won't kill the yeast (Unless it's below freezing), but it will slow way down, so feel free to throw the dough into the fridge but expect it to take longer to rise. Dough over 100 degrees will start to be problematic, as there is a chance the yeast will get baked to death. 70-90 degrees Fahrenheit is considered ideal.

before punching it down and letting it rise again. "Punching dough" sounds like jargon, but it isn't, you literally punch the dough until most of the air has escaped. While punching can be therapeutic, it's not obvious why it's necessary. To simplify, yeast is fickle and may or may not take well to your dough. It spends a little time tweaking the conditions of the dough[7] to its liking before it starts to rise, and depending on conditions it could take anywhere from 30 minutes to several hours to double. In some cases it may not double at all, in which case you'll have to throw your hands up in despair and try again when your pride has healed. Regardless, once the dough has proven that it has the capacity to double, punching it down and making it rise a second time will give you more evenly sized gas bubbles, the control of precisely when to put the dough in the oven, and the satisfaction that comes with beating up single-celled organisms.

Adding Air

If the point of using a leavening agent like baking soda or yeast is to introduce bubbles into our final product, why don't we just manually add bubbles to the dough itself? Actually, we already do. It's impossible to mix dry and wet ingredients together without incorporating a little air. Unfortunately, it's usually so little that it hardly contributes to the final

---

[7] Specifically, the CO_2 it produces first dissolves into the water and makes the dough slightly acidic, which yeast prefers. Depending on what kind of yeast you're using, it may also take a little while to "activate" out of hibernation.

leavened product, only sufficient for dense brownies and cookies. That said, bakers have a couple tricks up their sleeves when it comes to adding air to dough. The first is simply mixing the everliving *hell* out of a liquid dough and baking immediately. If you've ever seen a recipe tell you to beat a batter for several minutes, this may be what they're after. This still doesn't add a ton of air, so if we want even more, we can take advantage of some ingredient's amazing air-retention properties.

If you've ever eaten a meringue or had whipped cream on your pie, then you have already experienced the fluffy powers of cream and egg whites. Whipping both of these ingredients allows for an immense amount of air to be incorporated into a dough, which is exactly the technique used in angel food cakes, mousse, and souffles. Even dense pound cakes use a small amount of air-based leavening in the form of heavily beaten butter.

A good rule of thumb for whipping egg whites and whipping cream is to whip until they form droopy peaks when you pull your whisk out. This is called "soft peaks", and is a good middle ground for baking. More whipping can add more air as it reaches stiff peaks, but too much will cause the egg whites to clump and the cream to turn into butter. If you're having trouble whipping egg whites or the air in your whipped whites is escaping too quickly, a bit of acid helps the egg proteins hold more air before breaking and sugar helps it hold that air longer[8]. For cream,

---

[8] Acid is usually added in the form of cream of tartar, and you should only add the sugar once the whites are partially

make sure that you have whipping cream rather than light or heavy cream, and that the cream and mixing bowl are both cold. Whipping can be a fickle process, and it may seem like you'll never reach the soft peaks stage. While it's always possible that something went wrong[9], put another 5 minutes into heavy whipping (less if you're using an electric mixer) before throwing in the towel.

Steam Pockets

Steam? That's right, one of our leavening agents comes straight outta the 1700's. In general, a dough that has an uneven mixing of water and other ingredients is the mark of a chef so inexperienced as to have never read this book, but in some cases it can be useful to have pockets of water unevenly scattered through the dough. When it bakes those little pockets will vaporize, leaving behind little steam bubbles that force the dough to rise. The question is: how do we get uneven water distribution without looking like a total noob at baking? The most popular way is also one of the most delicious: Butter!

When butter is cold it can be difficult to fully mix into the dough[10], and we can take advantage of that

---

whipped.

[9] Some common problems include:

A bit of yolk in the whites (throw out and try again, the fat will prevent bubbles from forming)

Old eggs are harder to whip (add a tiny bit of acid)

Wrong kind of cream (honestly, that one is on you)

Wrong utensils (you should really get an extra large mixing bowl and a good whippy whisk)

[10] This is why cookie recipes will often have you "cream"

fact, either by kneading cold butter into the flour early on, or by shoving chunks of butter into our already formed dough before kneading carefully. This is a difficult technique to master, and can be messy (just ask my fully buttered countertop), but is the secret behind buttery croissants and flaky pie crusts.

Adding other ingredients

When you throw dough into the oven, hundreds of chemical reactions start. Some cause the crust to darken and acquire a shine, while others stretch the dough to its breaking point. It's impossible to discuss all of these in such a short book, but there are a few ingredients that can drastically change the product if you understand them. We'll focus on eggs, dairy products, sugar, and salt as some of the biggest influences.

Eggs

What happens when you cook an egg? It's not a trick question: it goes from a liquid to a jelly-like solid. It serves the same function in dough, as the dough heats the egg solidifies and the proteins add structure and springiness to the final product. If your pastry is too crumbly and you don't want to modify the recipe to increase gluten, eggs can replace some of the water and fat[11] in your recipe to tighten it up.

---

the butter and sugar together first, which will make it easier to incorporate into the dry ingredients. More on this in the Prep section.

[11] 100 grams of egg contains 11 grams of fat and 75 grams of

Alternatively, if your pastry is too springy, removing some egg can soften it. If you feel like getting more involved, remember that eggs can be separated into whites and yolks, with the whites having no fat and the yolks being ~25% fat by weight. Recipes that call for extra yolks are frequently trying to increase the fat content without sacrificing as much structure as adding oil directly.

Cream

Like eggs, dairy products contain both fat and water[12]. Additionally, dairy products usually contain protein that can toughen the final product, though to a lesser extent than eggs can. The biggest change when you use dairy products is one of taste. Only the most unobservant diner would miss the difference between biscuits made with buttermilk/heavy cream/butter and those made solely with water and oil.

Another thing to consider is that dairy products act as a "pH buffer", which is a technical term that I can't be bothered to study the chemistry of, but in short helps keep dough from getting too acidic or too basic. You might be thinking, "Why the hell do I need

---

water, along with 13 grams of protein.

[12] I recommend that you look up the specific values for whatever ingredients you're working with, but as a quick reference:

Whole Milk - 96% water and 3% fat
Light Cream - 75% water and 20% fat
Heavy Cream - 60% water and 35% fat
Butter - 20% water and 80% fat

to keep track of the pH of my dough? Does this asshole think I need a chemistry degree for *baking*?!?". Thinking about pH is one of those things that rarely matters, but can be an absolute killer in the rare cases where it does. It's usually safe to ignore, but if things won't work out the way you want and you can't figure out why, try incorporating some dairy products as a corrective measure.

Sugar

Adding sugar to your dough can serve many purposes, but certain properties are only fully realized at certain concentrations. In small amounts (1-4%), sugar can give yeast a boost to proof and rise quicker, like giving espresso to a college student. It also slows the rate at which the proteins in egg and gluten set up, giving the dough extra time to rise in the oven (see the section on **oven spring**). As you add more sugar (enough to easily taste), it starts to latch onto the water in your dough, preventing it from being absorbed and used by the flour. This will make for a looser dough, and even in a sufficiently solid dough can limit the amount of gluten forming. The sugar will only release the water it's holding on to once it's heated, meaning that the center of your product will have more moisture once it's cooked, and it will take longer for crust to form. This effect is small but increases as you add more sugar, and at the level of cookies and cakes there won't be any crust formation at all.

Salt

All dough needs salt. In higher amounts it serves specific purposes, but even a pinch of salt (<1%) can serve as a flavor enhancer, and is always worth adding. It also has the property of strengthening gluten, adding salt to recipes can toughen the gluten network through the dough, helping it hold its shape. If your dough is slumping in the oven or sinking in the middle, an extra dash of salt (assuming that your dough isn't very low in gluten) might be all you need.

Salt has been used for millennia as a food preserver, in some cases to dry food into jerky or other goods, but in others it attacks harmful bacteria and fungi directly. A typical 2% solution of salt in bread dough is enough to delay malicious organisms, but while higher percentages delay them further the salt also limits the growth of any yeast in the dough, with 5% being enough to slow yeast to a crawl. Sometimes a slower rising process is desirable, as it gives the dough time to rest and for gluten to form, but if your dough is failing to rise in the time you want you may want to check that you're not adding too much salt.

Substitutions and the Simplest Recipe

Do you currently have all of the following in your pantry/fridge: whole milk, skim milk, buttermilk, evaporated milk, yogurt, light cream, heavy cream, whipping cream, sour cream, cream cheese, cornmeal, cornstarch, butter, margarine, shortening, lard, canola oil, olive oil, and eggs? Yeah, me neither. When faced with a recipe you don't have the ingredients for you *could* buy the exact ingredients you need, but you'll probably end up throwing the rest out once you realize that you have no use for it. Alternatively, you could try and substitute ingredients that are more to your taste and needs. That's what this section is all about.

So what makes one ingredient (or a combination of ingredients) an appropriate substitute for another? A different way to ask that question might be: when bakers substitute one ingredient for another, what stays the same with regards to the recipe, and what changes? The tool I found was to keep 3 values the same: how much water, how much fat, and how much other stuff (proteins, sugar, salt, etc.) is added to the flour. This **dough percentage** can be calculated with some simple math, and has the added benefit of helping me feel like my degree in mathematics will somehow be useful in my everyday life. Looking at a pizza dough recipe (from a random Google search) and working out the math, it called for 450 grams of flour, 350 grams of water, 28 grams of olive oil (which is 100% fat), along with 18 grams of other stuff (salt, yeast, and sugar). We divide each of those numbers by the amount of flour (450g) and get:

- Water: 77.8% of the flour weight (warm tap water)
- Fat: 6.2% of the flour weight (olive oil)
- Other ingredients: 4% of the flour weight (salt, yeast, and sugar)

These 3 numbers form the fundamental building blocks of how a dough will turn out. If you don't have any olive oil in the house, but like the idea of using butter in your dough instead, then you can see what would happen to those numbers if you replaced the 28g olive oil with butter. 28g of butter contains 23g of fat, 4.7g of water, and 0.3 g of other stuff (milk solids). Now the pizza dough recipe calls for 450 grams of flour, 354.7 grams of water, 23 grams of fat, along with 18.3 grams of other stuff (salt, yeast, sugar, and milk solids).

- Water: 78.8% of the flour weight (warm tap water and butter)
- Fat: 5.1% of the flour weight (butter)
- Other ingredients: 4.1% of the flour weight (salt, yeast, and sugar)

The new recipe looks almost the same as the old recipe, and honestly it's probably close enough that we won't be able to tell much of a difference. If we wanted to indulge our perfectionist tendencies we could decrease the amount of tap water slightly with a corresponding increase in the amount of butter to get even closer to the original percentages. Okay that was a pretty simple example, how about another? My wife loves popovers[13], so here's the dough percentage for her favorite popover recipe: 125g flour, 100g eggs

---

[13] Someone pointed out to me that a lot of people don't know what a popover is. I typically direct those people to Google.

(20g fat, 66g water, 14g other), 244g milk (8g fat, 216g water, 20g other), 13g shortening (100% fat), and 2g salt, giving us 41g of fat, 282g of water, and 36g of egg/milk proteins, sugars, and salt. If you didn't actually read through all those numbers, I don't blame you, but you'll have to trust me that adding them up (and dividing by the flour weight) gives the following percentages:

- Water: 225.6% (milk, eggs)
- Fat: 32.8% (milk, eggs, shortening)
- Other ingredients: 28.8% (milk, eggs, salt)

There is a lot more water in the popover recipe, and indeed the dough ends up like a thin pancake batter. There's also more fat in it, preventing too much gluten from forming which would keep the popovers from rising to their full potential. And now that I have the dough percentage, I can make a small batch just for her, or a giant batch for a huge dinner party (which I would *totally* do if I wasn't an introvert living in a one bedroom apartment) with minimal difficulty. Unfortunately some substitutions need to be made first. My wife and I don't drink milk but we have heavy cream for cooking, and we don't have any shortening but I like the taste of butter better anyway, so I should be able to find a combination of water, heavy cream, and butter that adds up to the same percentages. Changing out the milk for cream and the shortening for butter totals us 120g of fat, 206g of water, and 26.5g of other stuff.

- Water: 164.8% (cream, eggs, butter)
- Fat: 96% (cream, eggs, butter)
- Other ingredients: 21.2% (cream, eggs, butter, salt)

Well shit. That's a pretty drastic change from the original recipe. But now I can clearly see that I need less fat and more water, and I have several ways I can do that: I can use less cream and add more water, I can add more water and cut out the butter entirely, I can replace some of the cream with more eggs, or some combination of the above. While it's most important to the texture and baking properties to get the water and fat contents as close to the original as possible, the proteins and sugars in the "Other" category can also make a big impact on taste, the structure of the dough, and how the crust browns when baking, so I can't just outright ignore them. Here the amount of protein is a bit lower than the original (cream has more fat and less protein than milk), so once I get the water and fat contents close I can make some additional tweaks to bump up the protein content. The final recipe I ended up using used an extra egg white and some careful watering down of the cream.

For the more technically minded among you, this tool might be incredibly useful to keep in your toolbox, and has let me throw ingredients together on the fly with only the rough percentages to guide me. But if, perchance, this either seems like too much effort for too little gain, or you abhor the idea of doing *basic arithmetic* in the kitchen, feel free to leave this particular tool in the shed.

Making Preparations

Okay, you've got the ingredients and understand what purposes they serve in your recipe, what now? If you're naive enough to think that throwing every ingredient into a bowl and beating the hell out of it is the answer, you're in good company. In some cases that's not far off, but other times there are specific techniques that we need to consider to get the results we want.

Order matters

Is there any reason to mix certain ingredients together before adding others? To my surprise, the answer is absolutely. Sometimes the reasons are practical, sometimes chemical, sometimes mechanical, but there are reasons. If you don't have any idea what order to combine the ingredients, start by mixing all the dry ingredients together, all the wet ingredients together, then gradually add the dry ingredients into the wet ingredients. I've found this to work well enough for a lot of recipes, but there are some cases where you need to change that order.

Butter

When mixing butter into dough, it's usually mixed in cold to prevent the water, fat, and milk solids from separating. And while sometimes we want to use butter as a leavening agent and want to ensure an uneven distribution throughout the dough, we also don't want random buttery chunks in our cookies. There are two techniques pertaining to adding butter to dough: **cutting** in butter can give us larger pieces of butter scattered throughout dough (perfect for flaky pie crust), and **creaming** butter can ensure a more even mixture.

Cutting butter into a dough means that you add the butter to the flour (and sometimes other dry ingredients) first. Then you mix and squeeze and press, focusing on breaking up larger pieces of butter as you find them, until you have a slightly softened flour with pieces of butter scattered throughout. That's it. As with most techniques in this book, it's easier described than accomplished, but it's reasonably easy to tell from the finished product whether you broke the butter into too small of pieces or left them too large from the texture. As mentioned in the gluten section, mixing the butter in early on also helps limit the gluten that can form.

Creaming is the opposite of cutting. If we want the flour and butter to combine uniformly, we need to make the butter soft and "creamy" enough that it doesn't form clump. In theory you can do this by beating the hell out of room temperature butter until it starts getting fluffy with all the air beaten into it, but most recipes will have you beat the butter with other ingredients to help it along, especially sugar[14] or eggs.

Salt

In my experience salt is the most surprising ingredient who's addition can drastically change a dish. It's usually pretty easy, toss it in at the beginning and call it good, but remember that salt can ruin yeast's day if the concentration is too high. Salt isn't too harmful when mixed throughout the dough, but if you put the yeast and the salt in the bowl at the same time, letting them come into direct contact… Let's just say that it's no fun waiting for a dough to rise when you've accidentally murdered your leavening agent in the most brutal fashion possible: by sucking the water straight out of their cells.

Whipped ingredients

If you're making an angel food cake, meringue, or mousse, then you're using air as your leavener, whipped directly into one of your ingredients: egg whites, whipping cream, or butter. Air is the most fickle of leaveners, and likes to escape out the bathroom window when you're not looking, leaving you with crushed dreams and a fallen souffle. Consequently, it must be added at precisely the right time and with caution: right at the end and as gently as possible. You should have every ingredient

---

[14] Creaming butter and powdered sugar together also gives us a useful topping: Buttercream frosting! Add whipping cream to lighten it up and flavor to taste.

available, your oven preheated, and as much of the recipe complete before you start to whip your eggs, cream, or butter. That way, once they have been whipped to your liking you can incorporate them immediately, then put the dough directly into the oven, minimizing the risk of losing precious air.

Another trick to maximizing the air in liquid air-leavened doughs is to **fold** the dough when adding the airy ingredients. This is a technique where instead of simply beating or mixing the dough with a whisk or wooden spoon, you use a spatula to scrape along the front edge of the bowl and gently lift the spatula at the end to fold a portion of it into the center of the bowl. Rotate the bowl a little (so that you gradually scrape all sides), and continue until the ingredients look fully incorporated. This technique[15] preserves as many of the precious air bubbles as possible.

Roll it, fold it, cut it

Imagine how different eating a cinnamon roll would be if instead of being rolled into alternating layers of dough and cinnamon/sugar mix, it were rolled into a smooth ball with the cinnamon and sugar inside? Or if instead of a fluffy dinner roll rising outward from a ball of dough, it rose straight up from a flattened square? These kinds of things depend on how you form the dough before baking. I'm gonna ignore all the specific cases, there's no way I'm wasting time on how to roll a croissant, spin pizza

---

[15] If I've described this technique poorly, there are several videos on youtube that can show you the process in detail.

dough, or twist a pretzel. Instead, I'll go through some of the general steps that you most often see: rolling out, folding, stretching, and cutting. None of these apply to doughs that are too liquid/soft to hold their shape, in which case the only two techniques you need require little explanation: pouring dough into a baking dish, and scooping firmer dough onto a baking sheet or into a muffin tin.

Oh, and if you're doing your prepwork on a table, cutting board, or countertop, make sure to wipe down and dust the surface with flour to keep the dough from sticking. Future you will thank me when cleaning up.

So for whatever reason, you may need a large sheet of extremely flat dough, when what you have is a rounded lump of not-at-all-flat dough. What's an aspiring baker to do? The simple answer is to press on the dough just hard enough to make it flatter. Now that I've blown your mind with that revelation, we can talk specifics.

In cases where your dough is soft and low in gluten (like cream biscuits or scones), you can get the shape you want by pressing on the dough with the palm of your hand, focusing on the thickest portions of the dough. These cases are pretty straightforward, try not to overthink it. However, tougher doughs with higher gluten content have a springiness that will resist a simple press, forcing us to bring out the big guns: the rolling pin.

When you see people in movies using a rolling pin to flatten dough, all they're doing is pressing on the dough hard enough for it to deform. A rolling pin is firmer and stronger than the human hand, and can more easily persuade the dough to flatten. However, it will also stretch mostly in the direction that you're rolling, so if the dough needs to be square/round and is a bit oblong, rolling along the short axis will even it out. Rolling out dough with a rolling pin is harder than you might think, because if you *need* a rolling pin you're probably dealing with a high gluten dough. Every time you flatten it, it will give you a metaphorical middle finger by springing part of the way back to its original shape. Instead of succumbing to the justifiable rage you now feel at this obstinate lump of toughened flour, take a break. Partly to give yourself time to cool down, but also to let the dough relax. The more you work the dough the harder the gluten pulls it together, meaning that overworking a dough will make it tear before it can stretch. Giving the dough even 5 minutes can relax the dough enough for it to be workable again, though a longer break doesn't hurt either. Rolling out dough is a frustrating step to rush, so be deliberate in your rolling, take breaks when it gets overworked, and take comfort in the knowledge that any insults the dough throws your way will make the final product that much more satisfying.

Alternatively, some recipes call for you to stretch the dough instead of rolling it out. The most classic example of this is pizza dough, where a firm spin generates enough centrifugal force to stretch the dough away from the center. Honestly, I fail to see why this is superior to rolling dough out, except that it looks cool. While I admit that spinning and stretching dough makes you look "hella slick, bro" you should stick with rolling dough out unless there's a damn good reason for it.

Now that you've got your dough flattened, a lot of recipes will call for the dough to be folded, often many times. In part, this can be used to mix the dough if you added ingredients at a late stage, but more frequently folding serves to modify the way the product bakes and how the texture develops. Flattening dough aligns the gluten into a sheet instead of a jumbled network, and folding dough sets up the structure of the dough into layers of stretchy dough with far less gluten holding each layer together. This is the technique that makes some products flaky, with individual sheets of the dough separating from the others. In fact, products like croissants call for butter to be added between the layers to further weaken the hold one layer has on its neighbors. But even in relatively low gluten doughs folding can be useful. Gluten makes the dough more resistant to expanding, meaning that as you bake your dough it will mostly rise in the direction of weakest gluten.

A couple words of warning about folding dough: Just like with flattening the dough, it can become overworked and hard to fold further. Additionally, the only part of the dough that doesn't have well-aligned gluten sheets are the edges. The first is solved by giving the dough a rest while you sip a glass of wine, but the second can be tricky. If the purpose of your folding is to create layers and get a flaky texture then the exact orientation of those layers may not matter to you so much. But if you're trying to get a batch of scones to rise straight up, then you need to trim off the edges or they will rise unevenly and twist into delicious but hideous abominations. To minimize the amount of edge of your dough, you can flatten the dough a little more than strictly necessary before making the fold. You'll still need to cut some off, but the center of your dough will be better aligned the flatter the dough is when you flatten it.

Planning a crust

Okay, putting aside what your product tastes like, what do you want it to *look* like? Most of what people see when looking at a baked dish is the crust, the outermost layer. Should it be deep brown and shiny like a croissant or brioche? Golden brown and covered in huge cracks like a loaf of artisan bread? Paper thin and craggy like a perfect brownie? Or maybe they shouldn't have a crust at all, with the outside being as moist and soft as the rest, like a delicious carrot cake? Some of this depends on the choices you make when baking (as in, putting the dough into the oven), but for now we'll focus on the contributions that ingredients can play in the development of the crust, and what you can do during the prep phase to modify it.

Ingredient Contributions

For the most part, the portion of the dough that actually browns during baking are the proteins (which brown via Maillard reactions), and the sugars (which caramelize). All flour has a bit of protein and sugar in it, so you can expect a little browning as long as the dough gets hot enough, but adding sugar or high protein ingredients like milk and eggs can increase the browning that can occur.

Of course all that tells you how much browning is *possible*, you actually need to have a crust for it to brown. If (a) your dough is extremely wet, (b) has enough sugar that is holding tight to what water there is, or (c) you've added ingredients that release moisture slowly, the outside of the dough will stay moist enough to prevent the development of the crust. Sometimes that's just fine, but for a proper crust to form you may have to go back and modify the recipe.

Glaze

The crust develops on the outermost portion of the dough, so why don't we modify just that outer layer to give us the crust we want? The process of doing exactly that is called **glazing** the dough. Want the shiny brown croissant-like crust? That comes with a dough high in egg, so brush some egg yolk mixed with water over your dough right before baking! Want it darker but without the shininess of egg yolk? Try misting the dough with milk or cream. Butter does something similar, but the oil content softens the crust in case you don't like the idea of crusty dinner rolls. If you want a more caramel crust, switch from protein to caramelization, and spread some sugar (dissolved in a little water) over the top instead. Glazing can turn a simple baking project into a work of art!

But with great glazing power comes great crusty responsibility! Glazing is a fantastic technique to get a specific crust, but I classify it as a *modifier*, something that you can use to make a tweak or change *when you already know how it will turn out*. It's easy to say that an egg yolk glaze can make a crust darker, but darker than what? If no crust forms at all, then there's no crust to darken, and if the crust is already on the edge of burning than a glaze just adds fuel to the fire. Making beautifully glazed shiny pastries is a lot of fun, but must be done with caution, especially for people that might be lacking in baking knowledge (yeah, that probably means you).

Baking, finally...

Unless you enjoy eating raw dough and risking salmonella, at some point you're going to have to *bake* your dough. There are really only two main components of baking: How long do I cook it, and at what temperature? There are additional tricks and modifiers, but if you can figure out those two then you're 90% of the way there. Let's start with a few stupidly simple facts that will build the foundation of how to answer those two questions.

- Your dough can't get hotter than the oven it's in
- Certain chemical reactions only occur at certain temperatures
- Ovens heat the outside of the dough first
- It takes time for the outer portions of the dough to heat the interior of the dough
- When dough gets very hot, it starts to brown, then to burn

How long?

Just like cooking steak, dough has an ideal internal temperature that it needs to be cooked to. In hindsight this fact seems obvious to me, but it *revolutionized* the way that I bake. How do you know when a steak is medium-rare? You check to see if the internal temperature is ~145 degrees. An accomplished chef can tell the **doneness** with a poke and a glance, but the rest of us unexperienced goblins can use a meat thermometer. Same with baking.

175 degrees is the equivalent of a "rare" dough, where the dough starts to stiffen and is barely fully cooked, with 180-185 degrees being the "medium-rare" temperature for anything you want moist and soft. Once the dough reaches the boiling point of water[16] it's reached the "medium-well" stage and any additional cooking will start to dry out the dough. A few extra minutes and it will reach the chewy consistency we want in an artisan bread, but beyond that and we'll have entirely dried out the loaf like a steak that's reached the "well done" point.

In short, the answer to the question "how long do I cook my dough" is: cook it until it reaches the optimal internal temperature. Most recipes give a range of cooking times, not because they're being wishy-washy, but because *time doesn't matter*. What matters is doneness, and the recipe can't possibly know exactly when it will reach that point[17].

---

[16] The boiling point of water is 212 degrees at sea level. If you live at an altitude significantly above that you'll need to decrease the temperature by roughly 2 degrees F for every 1000 feet of elevation. I live in Denver, Colorado (~5000 feet) and would have a horribly dry loaf if I let it get up to 210 degrees (~8 degrees above water's boiling point here), and anyone living in Cusco, Peru should pull their bread out of the oven before it reaches 190 degrees.

[17] After all, that depends on how well your oven retains heat, whether air can easily circulate in your oven, the

How hot?

If dough can't get hotter than the oven it's in, and ovens heat dough from the outside, then by simple logic we can say that the temperature of the oven will directly affect the final temperature of the outside of the dough. Once the outside of the dough reaches the boiling point of water[18] the water in the dough will (shockingly) begin to boil off, giving us an outer crust. As that happens, the crust is slowly heating the layer of dough under it, which is in turn heating the dough further in, etc. This causes a delay in the cooking of the center of the dough, with a longer delay the less heat is applied. Consequently, the temperature really only affects two things: The formation of the crust, and the time until the center starts to heat.

It sounds stupid to define what the crust *is*, but it's worth stating specifically: The crust is the portion of the dough that has dried out. That's it. Determining what temperature to bake at means finding the balance point of what the crust will be like at the moment the correct internal temperature is reached. This frequently requires a bit of trial and error, but here are a few guidelines I find helpful:

- The longer the dough is in the oven, the longer the outside of the dough has to dry out, resulting in a thicker crust.

---

temperature of your dough, the humidity in the air, etc.

[18] Keep in mind that the boiling point of water varies at different altitudes, which is one reason why "high altitude" baking instructions exist.

- Higher temperatures give darker crusts.
  - If the oven is under ~310 degrees, minimal browning will occur.
  - From 310-350 degrees, proteins will start to brown (especially if using a high protein glaze).
  - Above 350 degrees sugars will also start to brown.
  - Consequently, there's a *huge* jump in browning between a 350 and 375 degree oven.

Anything else?

Getting from prepared dough to a baked final product is tricky business, and so far I've only given you two variables to play with, temp and time. While it's a good place to start, two variables doesn't really give you the freedom to bake something to perfection. But fear not! There are additional modifiers and tricks that can help you further control the baking process!

Oven Spring

When making bread, we let the dough rise before we put it in the oven, but the dough does a significant amount of rising during the baking process too! This oven spring occurs when the oven has heated up the dough enough to kick the yeast into overdrive, producing another burst of gasses that inflate the dough even more, as well as causing the already present gas to expand. If you've ever seen bread that had a craggy and cracked crust, that was caused by oven spring cracking what crust had formed early on.

In some cases, especially with hearth breads, we want to take full advantage of the oven spring, giving us as large and fluffy a loaf as possible. However, the baking process is working against us: as the dough bakes it forms a crust, which can sometimes be too stiff to allow further expansion of the dough. So what can we do to prevent the crust from keeping the dough from rising? One massively useful trick to delay the formation of the crust (but that still allows it to form eventually) is to keep the outer layer of the dough wet enough that it can't completely dry out. Toss a handful of ice cubes into the bottom of your oven and the oven will stay humid enough for the dough to stay slightly moist. Once the oven spring has ended (when the internal temperature is ~120 degrees), you can open the oven a crack to let the remaining steam escape and to let the crust form.

Retaining Heat

The hardest part for me about baking is the overwhelming temptation to have a quick peek in the oven to see how everything is going. This urge becomes unbearable when I'm making something new or modifying an existing recipe, as my fear of fucking it up at the last minute overpowers my self-control. Even worse, every time I open the door I can feel the heat escaping, making the oven temperature drop and delaying the baking of the dough. Being unwilling to go on a journey of self-growth and modify my own behavior, I found a workaround.

First, I could minimize how often I needed to check the dough. A temperature probe with a long cord let me monitor the internal temperature without opening the door, so all I needed to check on was the crust. A good scrub of the interior window and a nice bright internal light bulb let me see inside well enough to assuage my worst fears. Second, my degree in physics (still not worth the cost of tuition) taught me about the transfer of heat. While the hot air is the primary thing heating the dough, and it is this air that we lose when opening the door, we can heat the air back to temperature more quickly if there is a lot of additional mass in the oven. Specifically, I keep a large cast-iron skillet on the bottom rack of my oven as a heat reservoir[19], so that any time the door is opened and closed, the air can heat back up more quickly. Lastly, the longest time when the door of the oven is wide open is when we're loading the dough into the oven after preheating. This loses us a massive amount of heat right at the beginning of the baking process. Sometimes it isn't a bad thing to start off the oven at a lower temperature (like when maximizing oven spring), but if you want to start the dough off hot, preheat your oven to 25-50 degrees higher than you want it[20]. Then, once the dough is in the oven, turn it back down to the intended temperature.

---

[19] It takes a while for this reservoir to heat up, so once your oven is preheated wait an additional 5-10 minutes for the skillet to get just as hot as the rest of the oven.

[20] We're essentially playing off the inefficiency of heat transfer, and betting that when the oven cools, it cools down to where we wanted it anyway.

Changing temperatures

Related to intentionally overheating the oven when preheating, it can also be useful to change the temperature partway through the baking process. Remember that we need to time the crust we want with the proper internal temperature, and sometimes one gets ahead of the other. We'll handle each case separately.

What do you do if the crust of your dough is nice and dark, but the internal temp is too cool and you fear that if you keep cooking it you'll end up with a too-dark crust? Easy, turn down the temperature until it's cool enough that it can't brown any more. How low do you set it? That depends on how thick you want your crust. Going back to the "stupidly simple facts", if the interior of the dough is heated by layers further out then the lower the temperature is the longer it will take for the center to be heated and the more time the outer layers will have to dry out. I refer you back to the "how hot" section for what temperatures will and won't cause browning.

What if the opposite happens, and your dough is nearly up to temp but you want a darker crust on it? Another easy question, turn up the temperature to the point at which browning can occur faster, usually over 400 degrees. How high to go? That depends on how much time you think you have left. If you've got another 15 minutes to go and are just making a slight adjustment to darken the crust, a small 25 degree increase might be all you need. If it's only 5 minutes, crank up the temperature by 50-100 degrees, camp out in front of the oven looking for the faintest wisps of smoke, and don't open the oven and let any heat escape unless you absolutely need to. If all you have is sixty seconds until the center is perfect and you desperately need to darken up the crust, throw on the broiler and politely request aid from any nearby Pagan gods in return for a slice of whatever you're baking.

A couple of final notes. Having to change the temperature drastically is usually a sign that the initial temperature was incorrect[21]. If you can, add a note to the recipe so that you don't need to make wild adjustments partway through. It's also worth noting that if you're baking at a low temperature (~350 or lower) and are shooting for a lighter crust, this advice is mostly going to be unhelpful, and you'll be better off just trying to be patient and wait a goddamn minute for it to finish baking before jumping to conclusions.

Cookware

Another question I had growing up was: why are there so many baking dishes, cups, and pans? Does it matter? Turns out, my sweet naive past self, it does matter, and not for purely aesthetic reasons either. When trying to ensure that the interior of the dough reaches the optimal internal temperature at the same time as the crust (or lack thereof) attains the properties we want, one question arises that my younger self had never considered: how far away

---

[21] Some recipes do specifically call for a change in temperatures, usually to achieve some very specific properties of the crust.

from the crust is the "center" of the dough? If you're trying to bake a giant cookie in a mostly full casserole dish, the answer is <u>too damn far</u>. Alternatively, spreading a modicum of dough extremely thinly across a baking sheet is great for focaccia that's chewy and slightly dry all the way through, but either drastically limits the time for any crust to form or makes the entire product into nothing but crust. For another example, angel food cakes are extremely delicate and easy to overcook, which is why they are baked in tins that have a hole through the middle (if you're confused, Google a picture of one), allowing it to begin cooking from the "center" immediately.

That's not to say that you can't change up your baking pans from time to time, if you want to pour your cake batter into mini muffin tins by all means proceed! Just know that while the flavor will probably be similar, the texture, density, crust, and how much it rises could change as well. You may have to make adjustments to the recipe, oven temperature, and especially to the cooking time to accommodate the change, but hey, that's what this book is all about!

Making it my own

Sometimes we fuck it up. And by "we", I mean me. There's nothing so humbling as producing the worst looking and tasting brownie of your life, in the middle of writing a book on baking, and then having the audacity to be *proud* of that miserable excuse for a pastry. One night in a fit of insomnia and chocolate cravings, I decided to make a personal brownie in a shallow ramekin (or whatever they're called). Rather than reaching for a recipe (which I would have to reduce to a single serving) I thought it was a good opportunity to test what I'd learned while researching this book. I desired a challenge.

First, what did I want the final product to be like? I've had brownies that are so fluffy and thick that they're essentially chocolate cake, but I'd also had brownies that had the density and consistency of fudge. I wanted to shoot for something 70% of the way along the fudge side of the spectrum (I like a dense brownie). I also knew that I was going to be pouring the brownies into the ramekin (calling on my previous experience with boxed brownie batter), so I wanted a liquid dough. There was also the chance that this wouldn't go the way I wanted, so I needed to keep track of how much of each ingredient I was adding so I could modify the recipe and try again later.

To start, I added my flour to my mixing bowl, then based all my other ingredients as a percentage of that weight. I knew that cocoa powder was strong in flavor, but wasn't sure *how* strong, so I took a guess and added 50% the weight of the flour. To counteract the bitterness I added 100% weight of sugar, as well as a dash of salt. At this point I had to make the most important decision: leavening. Yeast would have taken longer than I wanted and probably would create a weird flavor for brownies, and neither mechanical nor steam leavening seemed like good fits for the product, so I went with baking powder as my chemical leavener. I wasn't sure how much to add, so I took another guess and added 10% the weight of the flour.

Once I had the dry ingredients mixed together it was time to add the wet ingredients. I knew that the final product shouldn't be tough, so I needed to make sure that I would be adding enough fat to the mix to prevent much gluten from forming. I also suspected that adding cream or butter as a source of fat might make the final product more like a dense chocolate biscuit than the brownie I was after, so instead I started with a single egg (120% the weight of the flour, this was a small batch after all...), and 50% the flour weight in oil. A few quick turns with my spatula let me know that that wasn't enough liquid to create the liquid dough I wanted, so I added water as I mixed (foolishly not tracking how much) until the dough was the thickness of chilled cream (slightly thinner than intended).

Not wanting a crust to develop, and knowing that I didn't have to worry about browning (how much browner can a brownie get?) I preheated my oven to 400 degrees. Once it was up to temp I poured my dough into my greased ramekin and popped it into the oven, not bothering with any special procedures like steaming (I wasn't facilitating any rising) or glazing (again, a brownie doesn't need a crust). Then I paced nervously around and around my kitchen at 1am while I waited for the internal temperature to reach 180 degrees (hot enough to set up, but still very moist).

The instant I took it out of the oven I knew I had made a mistake. The dough had risen more than I had intended, and after it had cooled a bit a gentle poke at the top revealed that it was surprisingly springy and resilient. Add to that the fact that the brownie was unpleasantly bitter with cocoa powder and I could confidently rule this as a failure. That said, I had enough knowledge to try and modify my original recipe and try again. I decided to make the following changes:

- Decrease the cocoa powder by half to improve flavor
- Use only the yolk instead of the whole egg to prevent the proteins in the egg from giving the brownie too much structure
- Decrease the baking powder by 75% to keep it from rising too much

There certainly could have been more changes, but

too many and I wouldn't know which change in the recipe had caused which change in result. I tried again the next morning (because brownies make for the best breakfast!) and was extremely pleased with the results. The cocoa flavor was no longer overwhelming, the brownie still rose but only about half as much, and the brownie didn't have that chewy springiness that I had attributed to the egg white. While it paled in comparison to my mother's brownie recipe, I was still proud that I had learned enough to successfully tweak a shitty recipe in the direction that I wanted.

The End of the Book

Well, that's it. That's all I got. There are dozens of other tips, techniques, and tricks[22] that could be useful that didn't make it in, and countless others that I don't know and probably never will. After all, I'm not a baker. I sincerely hope that you have found these tools useful in your baking, or at the very least found them interesting. However, I have one final tip that is the most important of all of them: just give it a go. Flour is incredibly cheap (especially if you buy a 20+ pound bag of it) so all you have to lose is your time. There's no shame in producing something less than ideal, or even something inedible, I certainly did. Screwing something up and trying to figure out what went wrong is the first and most important step to improving, both in baking and (at risk of sounding like an air-headed "Zen master") in life.

Best of luck and remember, there is no better stress relief than punching the ever-living hell out of risen dough.

---

[22] If you're interested, I recommend starting with:
Adding alcohol to pie crust dough
Fermenting a sourdough starter
Incorporating enzymes into dough
Utilizing other (non-wheat) flours
A lye "glaze" for making pretzel dough

Appendix: Allergy Substitutions

Making substitutions is one of the most complicated techniques in baking, and if you are allergic to some ingredients, substitution becomes of *vital* importance. This is a complex topic, but I wanted to include some guidelines on what changes to make for a few more common allergies.

I AM NOT A MEDICAL PROFESSIONAL.

I AM A DUDE WHO THOUGH IT WOULD BE COOL TO WRITE A BOOK ABOUT BAKING.

PLEASE DO YOUR OWN RESEARCH ON ANY SERIOUS ALLERGIES YOU HAVE.

AND IN THE NAME OF ALL THAT IS BUTTERY AND SWEET PLEASE BE CAREFUL.

Gluten

If you're lucky, and just want to cut back on the gluten a bit, then you can implement some of the gluten-inhibiting tricks I've mentioned before: extra fat in the dough, minimize kneading, use whole wheat or a low-gluten dough. Then if your dough needs additional structure you can try and build it back up with other high-protein ingredients like eggs. If you *aren't* lucky, and need to eliminate every last strand of gluten from your dough, then you absolutely need to replace all of the flour in the recipe with a non-gluten-forming flour (rice, almond, buckwheat, etc.), making sure to avoid wheat-adjacent grains like rye, barley, and oats, which have lower but non-negligible amounts of gluten-forming proteins.

Wheat

This book mostly assumes that you'll be working with wheat flour, but if you're allergic to wheat there are some alternatives that give similar results. The simplest is to change the variety of wheat you're working with, some people find that while all-purpose flour triggers their allergies, varieties like "spelt" flour don't. If that doesn't help, you can also try flour made from similar grains like rye, barley, and oats. These have different properties, and produce less gluten than wheat, but might be helpful for those with a wheat allergy.

Dairy

Dairy can be a big influencer in terms of taste, but otherwise doesn't really provide many specific properties to dough, so substitutions are relatively straightforward. It's almost always fine to replace the dairy in a recipe with a carefully measured replacement of water and fat, though the protein content of your dough may suffer a bit.

Eggs

Eggs are a tough ingredient to substitute for, because they are such powerful modifiers: they darken the crust, modify the flavor, add water *and* fat to a recipe, and provide structure in many recipes that may otherwise be lacking. The first three can be accounted for with other ingredients, but the last is the hard one. I only know of two ways to add structure to a dough without egg or gluten: Gelatin and pectin. Adding gelatin (the ingredient that gives Jello its bounce) to a dough is a weird idea, but it should provide your dough with some of the rubbery texture that eggs would without affecting flavor drastically. And if adding unflavored gelatin to your dough isn't your thing, pectin serves a similar function. You can buy pure pectin from the canning section of some stores, but it is also present in many fruits, especially acidic ones like crab apples, unripe plums, and citrus. By replacing some of the water and sugar in your dough with a tart applesauce, for example, the naturally occurring pectin and proteins will help to serve some of the functions that egg would. The obvious downside to this is that it only works with recipes that you don't mind tasting strongly of fruit.